Our Holidays

Celebrate Earth Day

Amy Hayes

Cavendish
Square

New York

Published in 2015 by Cavendish Square Publishing, LLC
243 5th Avenue, Suite 136, New York, NY 10016

First Edition

Website: cavendishsq.com

This publication represents the opinions and views of the author based on his or her personal experience, knowledge, and research. The information in this book serves as a general guide only. The author and publisher have used their best efforts in preparing this book and disclaim liability rising directly or indirectly from the use and application of this book.

CPSIA Compliance Information: Batch #WW15CSQ

All websites were available and accurate when this book was sent to press.

Library of Congress Cataloging-in-Publication Data

Hayes, Amy.
Celebrate Earth Day / Amy Hayes.
pages cm. — (Our holidays)
Includes index.
ISBN 978-1-50260-246-6 (hardcover) ISBN 978-1-50260-238-1 (paperback) ISBN 978-1-50260-254-1 (ebook)
1. Earth Day—Juvenile literature. I. Title.

GE195.5.H39 2015
394.262—dc23

2014032629

Senior Copy Editor: Wendy A. Reynolds
Art Director: Jeffrey Talbot
Designer: Joseph Macri
Senior Production Manager: Jennifer Ryder-Talbot
Production Editor: David McNamara
Photo Researcher: J8 Media

The photographs in this book are used by permission and through the courtesy of:
Cover photo by DonNichols/E+/Getty Images; Sergey Novikov/Shutterstock.com, 5; NASA/File:Earth Western Hemisphere.jpg/Wikimedia Commons, 7; Joseph Macri for Cavendish Square, 9; Daniel Grill/Getty Images, 11; Jupiterimages/Stockbyte/Getty Image, 13; ivandzyuba/iStock/Thinkstock, 15; kali9/E+/Getty Images, 17; Yobro10/iStock/Thinkstock, 19; SerrNovik/iStock/Getty Image, 21.

Printed in the United States of America

Contents

Today is **Earth** Day!

Earth Day is a day that reminds us to **protect** our **environment**.

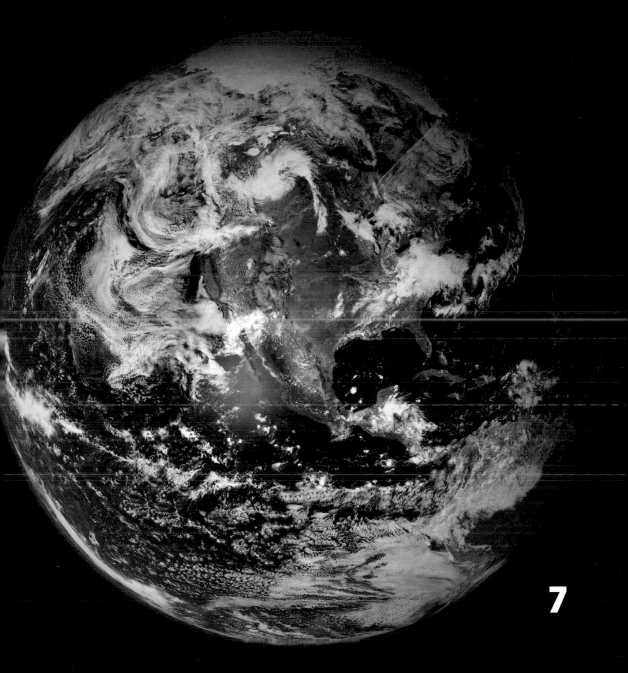

7

April 22 is Earth Day.

Today is April 22.

APRIL

Sunday	Monday	Tuesday	Wednesday	Thursday	Friday	Saturday
			1	2	3	4
5	6	7	8	9	10	11
12	13	14	15	16	17	18
19	20	21	22	23	24	25
26	27	28	29	30		

9

On Earth Day we try to help the Earth.

One way to help the Earth is to **recycle**.

11

We recycle plastic and paper.

We even recycle metal.

We also plant **gardens** on Earth Day.

We will need some gardening tools.

15

We help our teacher plant a garden.

Alicia helps in the garden.

She plants a pepper plant.

19

When we are done we play outside.

Happy Earth Day!

New Words

Earth (ERTH) The planet that we live on.

environment (en-VY-ron-ment) The soil, climate, and living things that affect a community.

gardens (GAR-denz) Plots of ground where plants such as flowers are grown.

protect (pro-TEKT) To keep something or someone safe.

recycle (re-SY-cle) To send something to a place where it can be made into something new.

Index

About the Author

Amy Hayes lives in the beautiful city of Buffalo. She celebrates Earth Day by recycling and helping the environment.

About BOOKWORMS

Bookworms help independent readers gain reading confidence through high-frequency words, simple sentences, and strong picture/text support. Each book explores a concept that helps children relate what they read to the world they live in.